CYNTHIA TIGNER

MIDNIGHT TO GLORY

My Purpose Almost Died

First published by Works Of His Hands Self-Publishing Consultant 2019

Copyright © 2019 by Cynthia Tigner

All rights reserved. No part of this publication may be reproduced, stored or transmitted in any form or by any means, electronic, mechanical, photocopying, recording, scanning, or otherwise without written permission from the publisher. It is illegal to copy this book, post it to a website, or distribute it by any other means without permission.

MIDNIGHT TO GLORY

My Purpose Almost Died.

PASTOR CYNTHIA TIGNER

Publisher: Cynthia Tigner

109 Wilson Ave Hinesville, GA 31313

Healing From Within Deliverance Outreach Ministry, Inc.

©2019 Pastor Cynthia Tigner

ISBN: 978-0-578-52051-3

Printed in the United States of America

Publishing Consultant: Delilah Varnum (www.theschoolofthemarketplace.com)

Cover Design: The Marketplace Strategist

Unless otherwise indicated scripture, quotations taken from the New King James Version Copyright © 1982 by Thomas Nelson, Inc. Used by permission.

Midnight To Glory – My Purpose Almost Died.

All Rights Reserved. No part of this book may be reproduced or transmitted in any form, or by any means, electronic or mechanical, including but not limited to photocopying, recording or by any information storage and retrieval system without permission in writing from the author.

First edition

ISBN: 978-0-578-52051-3

Proofreading by Celestine Vessel

I dedicate this book to my children Tamice, Tamika, Tichina (Keith) Mack, Tasean, and Tykeon Tigner for supporting me and believing in me. It was challenging, but we made it. My grandbabies, parents, grandparents, sisters, brothers, aunts, uncles, and cousins. I would also like to dedicate this book to my friends, my best friends, Deon, Michelle Daniel, Regina Lewis and Sharon, my God-brother Arice Brown, my God-sisters Kim and Tisha, Stephanie, and my "Ride or Die" Valanda Smith, Rest in Peace.

Contents

Preface	ii
Acknowledgement	v
LIFE OF A REBELLIOUS TEEN	1
Make the Bed You Lie In	1
OBEY YOUR PARENTS	6
Was He Crazy?	7
Know Your Worth	8
The First Tigner in History	8
THE LIFE OF A THUG GIRL	10
He's All Mine	10
I Wouldn't Hurt My Heartbeat	11
Everything That Looks Good	12
To Keep or Not To Keep	13
Touched	15
Running From Pain	16
2001 The Year My Life Changed	17
FOR THE LOVE OF MONEY	20
Favored With a Gift	21
Out of the Mouth of Babes	22
A New Women	24
SINGLE, SAVED, AND STRUGGLING	26
Healing From Within	26
Like a Fish	27
Delivered	29
ANSWERED THE CALL	31
About the Author	33

Preface

As I sit in my peaceful living room and reflect on my childhood memories and experiences it creates a sense of joy and pain. I can remember constantly moving from one household to another, attempting to get away from my granddaddy because he yelled and argued so much. I spent most of my childhood transitioning between the households of my cousin Diane, Auntie Gert, Auntie Beana, and Miss Buck. It didn't matter to me which household I resided in as long as I was not in the hostile environment that my grandfather created. He repeated the aggressive environment he experienced. *Men, you create the atmosphere for your family.* However, my grandfather was a hard worker and one of the best mechanics in Glennville, Georgia. He did not have an education, but he had many work skills. We appeared to be poor, but we never went without food, shelter, electricity, gas, or water. My grandfather was a provider. During the summers, he made us work at his mechanic shop or in the fields. He even made us pick up cans, and I was not happy about it. I really disliked working at the mechanic shop because we would leave with dirty clothes and smelling like motor oil. I was a little lazy girl, laugh out loud (lol). So I had lots of temper tantrums. I would leave and go stay with the inspiring women in my life. My summers were not like the typical kid experience. Looking back, my grandfather truly taught us how to survive.

When the summers are over, my life goes back to normal by hanging out at my favorite aunt's (Beana) house. I truly enjoyed living with her because she was more lenient than everyone else. She basically let me do whatever I wanted to. I remember her sweet humor as she would observe my bossy personality. One day, I was talking back to her husband with my hands on my hips, rocking my head side to side, and she would laugh. Her smile could light up a room. The love and care that she showed me was unparalleled to any other care that I had ever received from anybody, besides my mother. In Aunt Beana's eyes, I was the perfect little girl. She would always tell me that I was special, and she wanted me to feel a part of the family. Most of all, she taught me the word of God. One of the scriptures she taught me was "For God so loved the world, that he gave his only begotten Son, that whosoever believes in him should not perish, but have everlasting life." (John 3:16, KJV). Her favorite scripture was "Jesus answered and said unto him, Verily, verily, I say unto thee, except a man be born again; he cannot see the kingdom of God." (John 3:5-7, KJV). Some of my most cherished memories of Auntie was her taking me to church, the time she bought me an unforgettable black and white outfit with stripes, and sitting in a little red rocking chair in front of her TV watching the Trinity Broadcasting Network, a 24/7 Christian channel. My aunt was such a devoted person, she did Street Outreach Ministry by feeding the elderly and ministering to everyone she encountered. Whether a person was a drug dealer or on drugs, she still showed them unconditional love because she loved God's people. She was never ordained by man, but she obeyed God, did the work, and served His people. I used to assist her in her outreach ministry by feeding and taking food to the home of the sick and shut in.

    Unfortunately, one of the households I entered, I was molested by a man. The molestation happened more than once. I was seven or eight years old at the time of this occurrence. The man would physically come on to me in a sexual matter. He would lie me down on the bed and kiss all over me. I never said a word to anybody. I was clueless to what was taking place and did not understand at the time, but to be honest, the *touch* felt good. I blocked this incident out of my mind. Now that I am older, I look back at the situation, and I ask myself *why didn't I say anything to anybody?* I was young and not taught to tell if a man touched me inappropriately. I was unaware that my life was being shaped and changed forever. I was 10 years old when I started playing around and having sexual activity; we called it "hunching" in our day. I started playing hide-and-go-seek with boys as I began exploring my body. I know I was too young, but that man did this to me; he exposed me to physical touch. I had all kinds of sexual thoughts, not knowing that it came from the touching and kissing of a man that should not have been touching me at all. My innocence was taken, and the lust began. I was sneaky and very curious. I wanted more of that *touch*, and I didn't care whom I got it from.

Real Talk: **Parent(s) it is important that you know who is around your children, because the enemy will expose them to things that you never intended for them to experience. I was innocent, and he took from me what was pure. I found out years later that I wasn't the only one in the family molested. Then it became a generational curse. The enemy attached a spirit to me that took years for me to be delivered from. Never judge a person's life because you don't know their story. Parent(s) teach your children how important their body is to God.** "I beseech you therefore, brethren, by the mercies of God, that ye present your bodies a living sacrifice, holy, acceptable unto God, which is your reasonable service (Romans 12:1, KJV)." **Give your body to God!**

Acknowledgement

Writing my first book and finally getting it published has been a very rewarding process. I am thankful and grateful for all the people God has placed in my life to get me to completion. None of this would have been possible without my sister, Delilah. She is the woman who God set in my life as a covenant sister, friend and prayer partner. She is truly anointed for the Marketplace and I am thankful for our friendship.

I am grateful to my overseer Apostle Edward Futch and his wife Pastor Mary Futch. They are family by blood and by grace. They taught me discipline, tough love, manners, respect, and so much more that has helped me succeed in ministry. I truly have no idea where I would be if GOD had not set them in my life as my example. Thank You.

To my Mother my ROCK. Where would I be today if I hadn't had you during this time in my life and ministry. Your consistent support love and nurturing for me while I waited for the birth of this book has been unspeakable. Momma I love and thank you from the bottom of my heart.

To Pastor Tracie Wilkinson, you have been a Mentor and My Life Saver. Your wisdom has help me cross over some hard places in my life. I must say since 2012 you have been a Naomi to me.

To Vidual Futch, it was you who first spoke this book into existence. I bless GOD for your prophetic word and encouragement that pushed me to put my story in writing.

To China Mack, Thank you for helping me with my book and encouraging me. Momma love you. My personal school teacher.

To my church families: Healing From Within Deliverance Outreach Ministry (Hinesville), Deliverance Outreach Ministry of Macon and Glennville, and Woodbury Miracle Fellowship Center.

To my Facebook family and friends for your ongoing support I thank you.

Finally, to my future husband who was worth the wait. MY KING!

1

LIFE OF A REBELLIOUS TEEN

Make the Bed You Lie In

I grew up with a spirit of lust attached to me even though no one could see it. I wish my parents would have taken me to a Deliverance Ministry, somebody would have seen it. By the time I was eleven, I almost had sex with a guy. He tried to force it in, but I was afraid. Once I turned twelve, I started hanging out with a girl who was already having sex. She introduced me to her cousin, Bobby, and he wanted to have sex with me. He was so handsome, so of course I couldn't turn him down. She also told me it wouldn't hurt, and I fell for it. I started having sex nearly every day. I would skip school to have sex with him. When his mom left him at home, I would go over to her house and have sex with him. I was having sex with him like I was an adult. I was addicted to sex at the age of twelve. Once Bobby and I broke up, it didn't take long for me to get in another relationship.

In December of 1985 my secret was revealed. My mother found out that I was not a virgin anymore. My sister was pregnant and was craving pizza. My uncle looked at my mom and said, "you are buying her pizza, but you need to buy Cynt some". There was a sudden silence, and I looked at him like he was crazy; *dang he told my business*. My mom didn't exchange any words, and she took me to the doctor on the following Monday. That was the day that she found out that her thirteen-year-old daughter was pregnant. I was thirteen, in the 7th grade, pregnant. I was so ashamed, angry, and full of rage. I was more upset with the father of my child than anybody, but I should have been disappointed in myself. With me just discovering my pregnancy, he had the audacity to sleep with Monica, who called herself a friend. I was furious, so I never slept with him again.

During that time, my best friend died, and my first daughter, Tamice, was born. After having my baby, I started dating Bobby again. At this point, I was fourteen. We were back to the basics, having sex daily. *I loved this guy, but I lusted for many.*

By the age of sixteen, I became pregnant with my second daughter, Tamika, and this time she was Bobby's baby. I called her our "love child". Once my mother found out, she kicked me and my sister out the house because we were both on our second pregnancy. She put us in a trailer residence that my grandma owned. We knew it was wrong to keep having babies in our mama's house, but we did it anyways.

Real Talk: **My mom owed me nothing.** "Owe no man anything, but to love one another: for he that loveth another hath fulfilled the law" (Romans 13:8, KJV). I made my bed, so I had to lie in it. I disrespected this woman by having sex while being in her house. She took care of the first child, so I could go to school, but I turned around and had another one like it was the right thing to do. In life we need to be held accountable and take ownership of the choices we make. I had to grow up fast because I lied in a bed that I wasn't ready for "adulthood."

Am I ready for Adulthood?

My second pregnancy was so stressful. I did not receive any support from my child's father. Bobby cheated on me through the whole pregnancy, infidelity was his middle name. Sometimes I would stay with him at his mother's house, and he would disrespect me by bringing other females around. I should have been celebrating a sweet sixteen birthday party, but instead I was being a mom of two children, rebellious, and pretending to be an adult. I knew that I was too young to be going through so much, but it was the life I chose. Love is pain, right? My love for him was authentic; no one will ever love him like I did.

I fought all the time about Bobby; it was one girl after another. I even fought while I was pregnant with someone who was related to me. At the time, my self-esteem was very low, and I would do anything for Bobby. This young man was everything to me. He was my first love, *with his handsome self*. It felt wholesome to have a good-looking man in my life. He had my heart, mind, body, and soul. I considered him to be a trophy. All the girls wanted him, but it was something about me that would always keep him coming back. I was not the most faithful. There were times I would get with other guys. However, I always played the victim knowing I would cheat in a minute. Bobby had created a monster. My heart was cold, and I was spiteful. He kept sleeping with my cousin, so I would sleep with his cousin. Hurt people, hurt people, huh? That's how it was in the city I was raised in. Everybody sleeps with everybody, family too.

Real Talk: **Ladies, we can't do what men do.** I remember when Bobby told me that the girls in the streets would say that he looked too good to be with me. I never understood why he allowed those girls to make comments about me because it added fuel to my low self-esteem. My parents never told me that I was beautiful or loved, so I believed what those girls said about me. I received those words that were not true. I never knew what love looked like, so having sex and being mistreated was love to me. As a little girl, I needed to know that I was beautiful (tears flow as I write this). God has given me beauty for my ashes. "To appoint unto them that mourn in Zion, to give unto them beauty for ashes, the oil of joy for mourning, the garment of praise for the spirit of heaviness" (Isaiah 61:3, KJV).

Real Talk: "Danggggg! You are fine, thick, and your booty big (words boys would say)." I despised these words with a passion. I knew I had a big booty, but I wanted to be called beautiful, pretty, or gorgeous. **A girl needs to hear that she is loved and beautiful from her parent(s). No young lady should feel unloved or ugly. Parent(s) uplift your children, express your love to them, and show them what love look like.**

I never thought that I was beautiful, and as an adult; *the little girl in me cries even now to hear those words from my parents.* Bobby was young and didn't know any better. I have forgiven him and those girls.

Real Talk: **Ladies, never let a man belittle you, I don't care how much you think you love him.** You are a Queen! I dealt with situations I didn't have to, but I wanted to be loved. Remember, God loves you.

Finish the Race

No matter what came my way, I knew I was going to finish school. Even though I was a sixteen-year-old mother of two, I was determined to finish what I started. I missed many days from school lying in the bed with Bobby. He never motivated nor encouraged me to finish.

One early morning, I was asleep in the bed with him when I heard a small voice speaking to me saying, *go to school, he did not finish school.* I looked over at him, got up, and went to school.

Real Talk: **Ladies, always set goals, never let anyone stop you. Reach beyond the stars.**

I am Beautiful

One day I was visiting my uncle's amazing girlfriend at the time named Janice. She would take the time and talk to me about life. She was the first person to ever tell me that I was a beautiful young lady.

She always said encouraging things to me. She did not realize that God used her to build me up in an area where I was low. She helped heal my wound of low self-esteem. When she spoke to me, I openly accepted the things that she said. She showed me how to make myself look nice and taught me what my parents didn't teach me. I will never forget her, and I will always carry her in my heart. The words of inspiration that she spoke to me will always remain with me. *I will be happy when the day comes when women can see each other and say something nice without judging.*

Real Talk: **Ladies we have the power to change someone's life with the words we speak; encourage someone and give them hope.** "Iron sharpeneth iron; so a man sharpeneth the countenance of his friend. Proverbs 27:17, KJV)"

2

OBEY YOUR PARENTS

The time I turned seventeen years old, I started having sex with an older guy named Ricky. One night during our relationship Ricky saw me get out the car with Slim, whom I really liked. He waited on me like a stalker, grabbed me, and took me in the woods behind my grandparents' house. Ricky began beating me with a belt, and then he choked me. I blacked-out, and all I could see was stars as I fell to the ground. He started shaking me and attempting to bring me back to life. After I was conscious, he walked me to my mother's house as if nothing happened. From that day forth, I was afraid of him.

Another night, before my mother went to bed, she looked at me and told me not to leave her house. As soon as she went to sleep, Ricky pulled up, and I got in the car with him. *I ignored what she said because I couldn't tell him no.* He took me to a motel. Shortly after being there, his girlfriend knocked on the door, and he opened it. She charged through the door and hit him. After she hit him, she charged towards me, and smashed me in the forehead with a brick. Blood was leaking everywhere.

Real Talk: **Had I not disobeyed my mother, I would not be in this situation.** "Children, obey your parents in the Lord: for it is right. Honor thy father and mother (which is the first commandment with a promise) That it may be well with thee, and thou may live long on the earth" (Ephesians 6 1-3, KJV).

The enemy tried to kill me in my teenage years various times. I fought so much over Ricky. I was relieved when I got out of that relationship.

Was He Crazy?

Now I am back at it with Bobby. Of course, he is still the same olé Bobby. One day we had sex early in the day, and later that night he was with one of my family members in front of my face. Was he crazy? At this point, I was drunk and enraged, so I walked over to her side of the car and started a physical fight with her. I always carried a blade, so I pulled it out and cut her during our scuffle. She then grabbed the first thing that she touched, which was a screwdriver, and stabbed me in the face with it. The only thing that was crossing my mind at the time was death. I thought for sure that I would die. I stood there in shock, trying to figure out how the screwdriver was in my face.

I thank God for this man named Dwight. At the time, he was my God-sent angel. He calmed me down while saying, "You're not going to die". He spoke life when I thought death. "Death and life are in the power of the tongue: and they that love it shall eat the fruit thereof" (Proverbs 18:21, KJV).

My mom was home sick but praying. My cousin in law, Tam went with me on the ambulance to Reidsville Hospital. The doctors were clueless on how to remove the screwdriver, so they sent me to Savannah. When I arrived at the hospital in Savannah, the doctor said that I was an inch from dying, but God saved my life again. After we went through that situation, we never fought again. It took years for us to regain a relationship. I regret fighting her, and to this day I never apologized to her. I owe you an apology Mary. I apologize for fighting you that night. It wasn't your fault that he chose you over me. I love you and praying that we can continue building our relationship.

Know Your Worth

My teenage years were filled with plenty of fights and near-death experiences, but I am thankful that God had a plan for my life. God's plan is the reason why I am alive today. "For I know the thoughts that I think toward you, said the Lord, thoughts of peace, and not of evil, to give you an expected end" (Jeremiah 29:11, KJV). It was His grace and mercy that kept me. I took myself through so much pain, because I wanted Bobby more than life.

At eighteen, I became pregnant with my third child, Tichina. I was a senior in high school, and no one knew that I was with child. She was my "secret baby". I was not with Bobby at the time because he was dating another one of my family members. However, he wouldn't leave me alone. One day we all got in an argument, and she and I both had a knife. I cut her before she cut me, and I stabbed her on the arm. I almost went to prison for it, but God saved me once again.

Real Talk: **Ladies, when you don't know your worth, you will settle for less and let men mistreat you. WAKE UP!** You're a Queen, know your worth. Men will only do what you allow them to do.

Bobby was seen with me and slept with me on his terms, plus slept with other women too. The sad thing about that relationship is he treated all the other women better than he treated me. For example, he would take other girls on dates, but never took me on a date. He valued other women, and I was just the "baby mama."

The First Tigner in History

May of 1992 finally came as I was awaiting my graduation. What a year it was for me… as the first Tigner in the history of the Berry (Sallie Mae) Tigner's family to get a high school diploma. I was the young lady who got pregnant at thirteen and managed to finish high school.

This was a breathtaking event for my family. By the grace of God, I made it through. I thank God for the class of 1992 and faculty/staff members of Glennville High School. Especially Coach Waters, he gave me hope. I was happy that I was graduating, but miserable because my father did not attend.

There were people who doubted me along the way of completing high school, even some of my own family members. I put the work in, and God favored me. The night of my graduation, I could not go out and celebrate because of the bad choices that I had made. I stayed home because of warrant issues with me cutting my family member. The judge had presented me with orders that required me to stay home on graduation night.

3

THE LIFE OF A THUG GIRL

He's All Mine

When I was 19 years old, I was the mother of three beautiful girls while living in public housing. I thought I was doing something because I had my own place. It was a great feeling to have something that I could call my own. Going to college was not thought about at this point, but I should have gone.

The only thing on my mind was *Bobby*. I finally got Bobby to myself when he was in jail for drug charges. During his time in jail, he made me so many promises that he ended up not keeping. He was my heartbeat. I loved him so much I would have died for him. I waited on him to get out of jail for three months and it ended up being a waste of my time. I was faithful to him because he was the man that I wanted. He got out and cheated on me the same day! I was in so much pain and felt humiliated. The after effects of him cheating were devastating.

Bobby had opened an old wound, and I began to lose a lot of weight. I dropped from a size seven down to a size five in pants and went from 125 to 105 pounds. I had started drinking Ensure and eating as much as I could, but I couldn't gain weight. Nothing worked! I was in a bad place.

I told my best friend Rochelle that I needed to get pregnant because

I knew it would help me gain my weight back. In a few months, I was pregnant with my baby girl. I named her Tasean. She was my "planned baby". After I gave birth to her, I was so happy because I gained my weight back. I told myself that I would never let a man cause me weight issues again.

Real Talk: **I put too much trust in a one-sided relationship!** He didn't love me or treat me right. I was fighting for his heart that I had broken when we were younger. When a person doesn't have the heart to forgive you, they will hurt you over and over again. They will drag you down, but only if you allow it! Truth is: HE WASN'T MINE!

I Wouldn't Hurt My Heartbeat

I wasn't going to talk about this, but I must reveal the truth. During my pregnancy with Tasean, Bobby started talking out of his head. I had never heard him talk like that, so I called his mom. She said he was homesick because she and his brother had moved to Texas. Bobby was left behind with me and the girls, so I hit the local lotto numbers, and bought him a ticket to go to see his family. When he got there, he felt better.

I found out that the day he was getting on the train to come back to me, Bobby threw up. It was God's way of showing us that he needed to stay in Texas. Of course, none of us were saved, so we couldn't see the signs. He finally came back to Georgia, and I was excited about seeing the love of my life. Bobby got back in my house and got sick again. I had a preacher to come over and pray with him, but still nothing changed. I finally took him to a doctor, and they stated that he had a psychological disorder, and needed to go into a mental facility. I was infuriated because I knew they could give me more information, so I told the doctor he was foolish and left.

Out of desperation, we took him to a root worker. My grandfather always said, "if you go to a doctor and they can't help you, go see a root doctor." We drove him to the root doctor in Pembroke. People always said that he was the best. He told us that a man and woman put grave yard dirt in my yard and he walked over it and got sick. They were evil, and they wanted him dead. They did that to him because he was messing around with their teenage daughter. Bobby was dealing with so many young girls, so no one really knows which specific couple did it to him. We will never know the truth, but since I was the closest person to him, they said I did it to him. THAT'S A LIE! The person that did that to him was trying to kill him, and I would have never wanted to do that to him. They were dumb to think I would want to hurt my *heartbeat*. For years, I was angry and defending myself because I know I didn't do it. After all, Bobby left Georgia and moved to Texas. That was the day my life changed forever!

Everything That Looks Good

By the time I reached the age of 21, I had given birth to four daughters. My oldest Tamice was with my mom, Tamika was with her grandmother in Texas, and I moved to Brunswick with my God-sister. I brought my daughters, TiChina and TaSean, with me.

This city was full of sin, I must admit, I committed a lot of iniquities in that city. My life was full of partying, sex, and drugs. I liked one guy but slept with many. At this point, I just didn't care about anyone, and I had no values or morals. After the man that I loved left, it really affected me emotionally and mentally. I was still love searching; looking for love in all the wrong places.

Real Talk: **Ladies value your body and stop sleeping with men who care nothing about you.** When a guy can only see you on his time you're no value to him.

When I was in Brunswick, I smoked marijuana with my God-sister every day. I realized that smoking daily wasn't the life that I wanted to live, so eventually I stopped. My God-sister and I loved Miami. That was like our second home. Once, we traveled to Miami for a few days, and I met this guy through her friend. The two guys came back to Georgia, and I realized the one I met was outrageous! I was sitting in the car with him, and he wanted to have sex in the car. I told him that I don't do that anymore (I did in my teens). I was in my twenties and a little bit wiser. I didn't want to have sex with him at all. Once I refused sex, he got angry and pulled a gun out. I looked at him with fear in my eyes, and I told him that if he didn't let me go my god sister will bring my daughters to the car. *Why would you pull a gun out on a woman because she will not have sex with you?* Even then I knew God was watching over me.

TiChina and TaSean were in the house crying continuously. They cried so much that my God sister brought them to the car. God saved my life again by using my children. They were only two and three years old.

Real Talk: **Pay attention to your children.**

My babies were gifts from my womb. At this point, I knew that my dirty deeds were catching up with me. I learned that everything that looks good might not always be good for you!

To Keep or Not To Keep

The lessons I thought I learned, apparently, I didn't. I was dating three guys at the same time. While dating them, I became pregnant. I did not know who my child's father was, and I was thinking about getting rid of my unborn child. I was thinking *I am not going to have a baby by another man because I am with Bobby.* Yes, I was back with Bobby.

As I was in the process of moving to Texas, I was making plans to get rid of my unborn baby. Once I arrived, Bobby was sleeping with a female who lived down the street. It was a rough time for me. I felt like I was losing my mind. I was contemplating *I moved from my comfortability at home and sold all my possessions to deal with the same situation.* I was in a mental dilemma. Should I keep the baby and lose Bobby or get rid of my baby and still get mistreated? Well, I decided to keep the baby. Bobby had no idea that I was pregnant, but my heart was ready to accept the fact that we were finally over…At least I thought we would be.

The female from down the street was trying to fight and threaten me about Bobby. I would act as if it didn't affect me. When no one was around, I would go in the bathroom and cry while saying to myself, "I can't take it anymore".

The moment approached when he found out that I was pregnant and that it was not his… I was in the kitchen and his mama looked at me and said, "Cynt are you pregnant?" I responded "no" because I was planning to move out and get my own place. After a while, I had to tell him. He was mad and cursed me out. I mentioned my thought process on getting an abortion, however, since he was dating "the girl down the street", I kept my baby. He then told me to get out, but his mother told me that I didn't have to leave. I had nothing; no man nor a place to live. After we argued, I went upstairs, and I cried and prayed. I began to listen to the Mary J. Blige song "Cry No More", and I packed my things, gathered my children, and then caught the first thing smoking out of Texas.

I was so confused because he had children outside our relationship while he was with me, but when I did it to him, I was considered wrong.

Real Talk: **Ladies, men think that it is ok when they make mistakes, but when the shoe is on the other foot, they think otherwise.** Don't ever put all of your eggs in one basket. We as women give these men our all and end up with nothing in return. Stand your ground!

When arriving back in Georgia, everybody was amazed because my stomach was showing. Everyone knew that it was not Bobby's child, and at first, I was ashamed, but then I realized that I had nothing to be ashamed of. "Let me not be ashamed, O LORD; for I have called upon thee: let the wicked be ashamed, *and* let them be silent in the grave (Psalm 31:17, KJV)."

I loved a man that was not ready to love me back. After this, I never looked back!

Touched

I was finally back at my mom's house. I went to the doctor and discovered that I was having a baby boy. I started crying as I thought about my stupid plan to get rid of my child for a man who did not care about me. I was foolish for even considering that option. It is not good to place a man's feeling, before the life of an unborn child. I birthed a good-looking son and I chose to name him Tykeon.

After his birth, I was selling drugs to survive. Life was good. I was living with my mom and stepfather and living life with my children. One day we received a knock at the door, and it was Department of Family Children Services (DFCS). They mentioned that my child stated that she had been touched by a family member. I was in total shock, and my heart was crushed. DFCS requested that me and my children leave the house. I quickly relocated to the house of another family member. When I look back on the situation, it was the hardest day of my life. I value family, and on this day, my family was destroyed. I thank God that we all got passed it.

After this, we moved to Thomaston, Georgia. We moved there on a Monday and I had a job by Wednesday. I was truly grateful for the faithfulness of God. I knew it was the place that I needed to be.

Being in Thomaston taught me how to become a woman and a loving mother because I didn't have my mom there to cook and babysit. Therefore, I had to grow up and take care of my babies.

Running From Pain

I moved from one evil city to another. It wasn't long before I met and started dating a thug named Mike. He had money, but he was no good. I was a street girl, always looking for a doctor (someone to heal my pain). I was advised by someone I consider the best, my god-brother. He had always told me to never give a dude anything for free, only deal with a guy that has something to give.

It did not take long for trouble to follow me. I had only been in Thomaston for a week, and the drama had already begun. My cousin was having a cookout and a young lady came to fight me about her child's father. She thought he liked me, and little did she know, I was looking at his brother lol. I thought *wow, these chicks are doing things that I did when I was a teenager.* I wasn't afraid when the girl approached us; I wasn't the one talking to him anyway.

News about the incident had made its way back to my mom. Of course, she was fussing, but I still didn't care. Did I really learn my lesson from being a rebellious teenager?

Within two months, I was in my own house with Mike's help, but eventually, I had to let Mike go because he was too controlling. Then, I became best friends with a lady name Regina Lewis and we are still besties today. We always did adventurous things together. We were at a good place in our lives. We were young and having fun. Regina hooked me up with this guy, and he thought everything was a joke. We dated for a while, and he tried to play me, so I had to let him go. I didn't have enough love in my heart for him. The only good thing he did for me was run a stalker away lol.

One day, I was on my way to work when I decided to stop by Church's Chicken. I was going to see my cousin at her job and these guys pulled up. "Who are they?" I asked my cousin. Then she asked them where they were from and they replied, "Woodbury". She made a rude comment towards them, but I did not care because all I saw was money.

The guys placed an order for an apple pie, and once it was ready, I took it to them. Suddenly, a nice-looking guy with tattoos named Brad got out the car on the passenger side. I looked at him from head to toe and said "wow". At that moment, we decided to hookup, but I should have known not to deal with him. He was eye candy, and I knew he couldn't be single. When we had our first date, he took me to his city where they were having a block party. A female approached us and tried to fight me. Here we go again! I couldn't do anything but laugh, of course I didn't care. He had style, and I wanted him.

I had never given any guy my heart, except Bobby. Any other guy was a joke to me. I gave fake love to them while I was with them, and once it was over, I moved to the next. It was something different about this guy. I was head over hills for him. I would take whatever drama came with him. I knew he was no good. Here I was again, willing to fight over a no good man. He was everything to me. I thought I could not live without him.

I know you may be thinking, why him…Why not him? He spoiled me and showered me with gifts like no other. I didn't have to ask him for money, he would just give it to me. Plus, he was so sexy, he belonged in somebody's magazine. Although I knew he did his own thing, I was still sneaky too. We went through many situations, so eventually we separated. I was horrible after the breakup, so I moved back to Glennville. I ran home to get away from reality. I always blocked my pain. I was not ready to face my issues.

Real Talk: **Running away from your problems will never heal your pain.** Release whatever issues you have. Let it go so you can be healed.

2001 The Year My Life Changed

The year 2001 was filled with many good/bad things for me. I remember bringing in the New Year at my mom's house. After midnight, I went to the club. I had no idea that it would be my last

New Year's Party.

A few days later, my god-sister, Tot, Stephanie, and I headed to Daytona and we had a blast! We were staying at the best hotel in Daytona. It was nothing but top-notch guys and females in that spot. The rooms were very expensive, and it was considered the hotel to be at! That was the best vacation ever! We met a lot of famous rappers, and we took all kinds of pictures with them. More like, the best year ever!

When the summer came, I was planning my big 28th birthday celebration. I held it at a place big enough to hold the crowd that I invited, plus more. I was very popular, so most girls hated me and most guys loved me. I was always surrounded by guys. At times, they were better friends to me than females.

July 24, 2001 came around, and I was ready to party. I had on a red dress that cost $500.00 and my heels cost $100.00. My girl Pasha had done my hair and you couldn't tell me anything. I was too charming.

My special guests were; my god brothers Arice, Rondel, Boo, Bruce, Mark, Tellas, Dom P, and the whole "Ville". If you weren't at that party, you missed a good one. All of my ride-or-die chicks were there; Londa, Pam, Chelle, Pasha, and Tasha. That night even brought out the haters. *It's funny; they don't like you but show up to your party.* One chick was in the bathroom talking about me, and my god- sister heard her, lol. I was the life of the party, and I had no need to sweat anybody. It was my show, my spotlight.

After heading home from a successful party, I couldn't choose between the two guys that I was messing around with. Therefore, I went home alone. It was weird how I would always laugh, be happy, and entertain people when I was with a crowd, but when I left the crowd and went home, I was sad and lonely.

No matter how many men I dated or the number of friends I had, my life was empty. I was empty because I didn't have Jesus Christ as my personal savior. My heart longed for something called love.

Real Talk: **A man can only please you for a moment.** No man will ever do you like Jesus. If you're looking for man to make you happy and give you peace, he can't, unless he knows Jesus.

4

FOR THE LOVE OF MONEY

It was now the fall season, and I had moved to Hinesville, Georgia. Bobby came to town, and I only slept with him to prove a point to all the chicks in the Ville. Bobby would never leave me alone. *Who could fill this emptiness quicker than Bobby?*

One day, I was in school to get my certified nursing assistant license, and I received a phone call. Guess who? It was Brad. We hooked up, and I started making plans to move back to Thomaston.

It seemed like it was a part of God's plan because someone had called the Department of Family and Children Services (DFACS) on me while I was deciding on whether I would stay in Hinesville or move back to Thomaston. This situation was confirmation for me, so I left in October of 2001.

I got back with Brad, and he was still smooth and sexy. He was back to giving me money, and I was back to being in love with him. Although I was independent, Brad took care of me.

Real Talk: **Ladies it's ok to be independent, but remember, we are the helpmeet.** "And the LORD God said, *It is* not good that the man should be alone; I will make him an help meet for him (Genesis 2:18, KJV)." In Hebrew, helpmeet means "ezer" which means "rescue". Men don't come to rescue us, women come to rescue them. A husband is to love his wife just as Christ loved the church. Men in the world owe you nothing, so don't expect them to do what a husband would do. Hold your own.

Winter was approaching, and I was up to no good. I loved my man, but I loved money too. I was dating a guy named Tony while I was dating Brad. My heart belonged to Brad, but I loved the way Tony spent quality time with me. He was from Fort Myers, Florida. He was a great man with plenty of money. I couldn't let him go because he was wealthy. Money was the root of my problems, and money is the root of all evil. Being faithful wasn't on my mind. My mind was on **money**. "For the love of money is a root of all kinds of evil, for which some have strayed from the faith in their greediness and pierced themselves through with many sorrows (1 Timothy 6-10, KJV)."

Favored With a Gift

Soon after, I visited my mom and told her that I wanted to change my life. I always knew that I wanted to live a saved life. No matter what I did in those streets, I knew that I wouldn't stray. My Aunt Beana had paved the way. I would sit with my friends and smoke weed, and I would say "when I turn thirty years old, I'll be saved." They would laugh at my statement in disbelief.

The year 2001 was coming to an end, and God showed me that I was a motivational speaker. I was going to schools teaching and talking to the youth. Even when I was up to no good, God chose to favor me with a gift. "For the gifts and calling of God are without repentance." (Romans 11:29, KJV). I was totally amazed because I could really see myself teaching the youth. A lady in our neighborhood always said that God was going to use me one day. She saw the calling on my life.

In the month of December 2001, I took a HIV test. In the process of waiting for it to come back the enemy ran my mind crazy. The enemy was saying to me, "You know you have it, look at the lifestyle you're living." To be honest, it scared me like crazy.

I knew that I was going through something spiritually significant. I truly believe that God will speak to a person anywhere; we just have to listen. I would be in the club, and God would be speaking to me. Yes, he speaks to sinners and answers their prayers. He would also speak to me through other people. I worked at a nursing home, and one old lady, in her nineties, spoke into my life. She said, "God is putting another star on your crown". It scared me because I didn't understand what she was saying. I thought I was going to die. Tears dropped as she talked about God giving me a crown of glory. Now, I understand.

During that time, I had switched schedules with a co-worker because there was a big party happening in Claxton, Georgia the following Saturday. They threw some of the best parties in that city, so I wasn't trying to miss it. As I was preparing to go out of town, the thought of dying crossed my mind. I feared death, because I knew of God, but I was not ready to surrender my life to him. I also knew that hell would have been my home according to the life I was living. I thank God for the crown.

Real Talk: **Living in the streets was everything to me. No rules, No morals, No heart, and living reckless with no cares in the world.**

Out of the Mouth of Babes

On December 22, 2001 Mia and I were packing and getting ready to head home for the big party. Mia was my little sister who I train to know the streets. She was living around Thomaston too, so she would travel with me to our hometown. We were excited to go back home because we're small town superstars.

As we were traveling, we made a stop in Macon, Georgia to pick up my younger cousin, Vidual Futch. He was a preacher and a prophet at seven years old. Without a care, I was playing my favorite song at the time by Khia (My Neck, My Back), and Vidual said, "Cynt, you need to be saved." I was totally amazed. While laughing at his comment, I turned the music down. I was in total shock the whole way to Glennville, and the car became silent. All I could think about was what he said. Out of the mouth of a babe, I received a spoken word from God. I knew it was time for a change!

Real Talk: **Be careful of what you expose children to, especially someone else's child.**

When I made it to Glennville, I was exhausted from traveling. I went to my cousin Pam's house and fell asleep. Everyone was calling me to get ready for the party. It was outside the norm for me to turn down a good party with expensive drinks and party pills, but I did that night. As I was lying in bed, I tossed and turned the whole night.

I didn't know what was going to happen the next day, but I woke up with a mind to go to church. Before going to church, I wanted to visit some folks to discuss the new gossip and details on the party. When I got back, I looked at the time and said, "I can't go to church at 12:30 when it ends at 1:30". My cousin Pam looked at me and replied, "it's better to go late than to not go at all". Then I begin to get ready.

When I got to church, my mom, grandmother, and my loving Auntie were there. I sat at the back of the church. The young man that was hosting the service looked at me and asked, "Do you want some Christmas?" I replied "yes." He asked me the same question again, and again I said yes. I went up to the altar, and the next thing I knew, I was giving my life to the Lord. I immediately began to break down and cry because I wanted to give God my all. I told the Pastor of the church that I had no problem being saved, but I loved my boyfriend. The Pastor then prayed for us. I felt so good giving my life to God. A peace came over me, and I was filled with a great joy.

I have always told people that God tricked me, lol. God knew if that young man would have asked me do I want to be saved, I would have rejected God. However, I wasn't in the position to reject God because I had this feeling and sense of urgency that if I didn't get it together, I would die.

On that night, I went to my grandparents' house, the Kings, for a Christmas party. I knew my life had changed because I never would have gone to their house, if I wasn't saved. My daddy's family wanted the best for me, but I could not see that, until I got saved. In my carnal mind, I thought they were too good for me. I felt like I didn't belong to a family who was saved and educated with morals. The enemy had me blind, but salvation opened my eyes.

A New Women

I was heading back to Thomaston a new woman. I wanted to call my boyfriend and inform him that I was saved now, but I waited some days before I told him. My mom went back to Thomaston with me. I was so glad that she traveled back with me because the HIV test results were getting ready to come back. I knew I would need her to comfort me while waiting on the results. I honestly had no clue what the outcome would be. God showed his grace and mercy, and I cried because the test results were negative. What the devil meant for evil, God turned it out for my good.

After the test came back, I wanted to tell Brad that I couldn't have sex with him anymore because I was saved. Of course, that isn't how the situation went because I was weak for that man. I desired him so much that I made him my god. If only he knew. Our relationship was so addictive. I felt secure. I had God, *the man of my dreams*, and my children. I couldn't have asked for anything more. I thought I had the world.

I started school in January of 2002 for Early Childhood Education and still worked at night. My life was busy, but I was happy. The fall of 2002, Brad asked me to marry him. I was in disbelief, but I was the happiest female in the world. *My ring was so beautiful.* It was a nice one-and-a-half carat ring. On the other hand, we really didn't get a chance to enjoy our engagement, because some things went on during that time. Every time we would try and mend our relationship, it would feel different. I desired to be saved and do right by God, and I couldn't do that by being with him.

February 14, 2003, we had the best Valentine's Day ever. He bought me a diamond, tennis bracelet and necklace. I bought him diamond earrings. Even though love was in the air, I wanted a marriage, not just material things and sex. He was not ready for marriage, and I did not force him.

He called the engagement off by the summer, and I cried for days. I held on to him emotionally for years even though I caught him in bed with another woman. I craved this man.

Real Talk: **You can pray, cry, and scream all you want, when it's not the will of God, it won't work.** My faith couldn't convince God to give him to me. It was not God's will for us to be together. No matter how much a woman loves a man he must love you in order for you to see growth and a future.

5

SINGLE, SAVED, AND STRUGGLING

Healing From Within

I made a choice to follow God and it cost me everything. Although I was now living life saved, I was also single and struggling. It didn't feel good at all. I was working two jobs trying to make ends meet. I went from one relationship to another. I lowered my standards so many times to please the flesh, which is no good to us. I messed up over and over and it seemed like I would never be delivered from lust.

December of 2009, I was fed up with all the men that were in my life. I had been engaged again and was disappointed once again. My life was full of pain and rejection in the area of relationships. I was good enough to sleep with, but not good enough to be a wife. I thought that something was wrong with me from the way that men had previously treated me. I needed to be loved, and the love that I needed was in God and from God.

One day, God gave me a vision for a conference called "Healing FromWithin". It was for people that needed a healing from the inside. The conference brought many churches together in unity. I was not the only one that needed to be healed, there were others as well.

Even after the conference, I had iniquities that I was facing. I couldn't get it together. After eight years of messing up on God, I was still in a bad place. The spirit of lust and perversion had me looking at any kind of man like he was the one, but that was not the case. The enemy was putting traps out there for me, and I couldn't see it because of my flesh.

God gives us a choice. I made the choice to sleep around like I did before I gave my life to God and lust continued to follow me. That spirit was going to be my downfall if I didn't make a change. I did not understand why I could quit clubbing, smoking, and using profanity, but I couldn't break from having sex. It was like a drug addiction, once I started it, I couldn't stop. At this time, I would only sleep with guys that I was dating, not just anybody. I had been having sex since the age of twelve, and I needed deliverance.

Real Talk: **Just because you are saved, doesn't mean you are delivered.**

Like a Fish

In the summer of 2010, I was finally in a good place. I didn't want a man; I just wanted church, work, and my children. In June 2010, a friend of mine called me and asked me to be a friend to a guy named Deon. At first, I said "no." He was in prison and I had already been through a similar situation before. I didn't want to go that route again. Most men in prison lie. They use you until they get out, and then they forget about you.

After Bobby went to jail, I said I would never date a guy in prison. Soon after, I heard a small voice say, "Everybody needs a friend." So, I opened my spirit to Deon as a friend. We grew closer by emailing and talking on the phone. The next thing I knew, we were engaged and soon to get married. He was the apple of my eye.

My Bishop told me not to marry him yet and instructed me to wait until he got out. Of course, my strong-willed, rebellious self, married him anyway. God gave me a good Shephard, but I just didn't listen and got hurt and disappointed in the process. It was all about me and the things that I wanted. I couldn't see the bigger picture. I only saw that I didn't have to worry about having sex again because he was in jail. I had convinced myself that I was strong and free of lust and fornication. Yet, being married does not make you free from those fleshly spirits.

I married because I was selfish. My pride caused me to hit rock bottom before I was able to see my wrong. Now that I can see with a clear vision, I see where God was working on me. *I was like a fish.* God scaled me first and cleaned my outside. Then he had to gut me from within. He had to cleanse me from the sin that was corrupting me. Everything about Cynthia Tigner had to go so the Holy Spirit could come and live on the inside. He had to show me that I would never have anything if I kept making life about myself.

See it Through

2012 was a year that I will never forget. Deon called the marriage off, and I was devastated. I cried for three days straight. I received his wedding band back in the mail, and I had a phone call. The person on the line was laughing as they asked, "did you get your ring?" I couldn't believe that a woman would laugh at another woman's pain.

Real Talk: **Be careful who you laugh at.** You will reap what you sow when you are being cruel to people who did nothing to you.

My daughters, China and Sean supported me through this process. They were the only persons that I could trust and inform at the time. I kept it a secret from everyone else. "Be not deceived; God is not mocked: for whatsoever a man soweth, that shall he also reap (Galatians 6:7, KJV)."

Delivered

May 25, 2012 was a bittersweet day. It was my last day working at a job I loved at Upson County Pre-k. I had no idea where I was going, but I knew God had a plan. My family was in town, for my baby girl's high school graduation, and I needed my family with all that was going on.

My sister mentioned a child care job in Hinesville, Georgia, so I talked to the Pastor of the daycare. It was confirmation for me to leave Thomaston. I started the job in Hinesville on June 12, 2012. It was unexpected, but God sent me back near home. God had an assignment for me.

During this time, Deon would call me with drama, but I was over the foolishness. He would call and say things to upset me and we would go back and forth sometimes. He was living in the house with his baby mama, but calling me with drama. Finally, I said enough is enough because he cussed me out, and I had a problem with that. It opened a wound that I harbored. It reminded me of my grandfather fussing at me. I told God that day I don't desire Deon and I meant it. I had neither hope nor faith.

The more he called, the more anger and rage I felt towards him. "Put on the whole armor of God, that ye may be able to stand against the wiles of the devil. For we wrestle not against flesh and blood, but against principalities, against powers, against the rulers of the darkness of this world, against spiritual wickedness in high places." (Ephesians 6:11-12, KJV). I fought in the flesh and I didn't win. I knew God put that man in my life for a purpose, but my flesh, pain, anger, and rage cost me my marriage.

The summer of 2012, I got a prophesy that I was called to ministry. I was amazed by Prophet Outlaw Lewis, she was on point, and I took that prophesy to heart. November 2012, I talked to my leader and told him what God was speaking to me. He told me to humble myself and finish the ministers' class. For the first time in my life, I humbled myself and did not get upset and depart from the church. I waited on the appointed time of my release.

December 2012, I received another prophesy from another prophet, one I never saw before. He walked up to me and said, "God said don't worry about the people, get the paperwork completed." I prayed and asked God, "What do I do when I know you're calling me, but my leaders said stay humble?" After I prayed, I had a dream that I was leaving my church of 11 years. It was bittersweet, but I had to obey God.

In January of 2013, I left the church that taught me, loved me, and support me and my children. Then I joined another ministry, and my whole world turned upside down. I had to face spirits that I never knew were there, but God put me in a place so that I can see myself and be delivered.

Real Talk: **Don't let the devil fool you, obey God and do what our Father asks of you.** "And Samuel said, Hath the LORD *as great* delight in burnt offerings and sacrifices, as in obeying the voice of the LORD? Behold, to obey *is* better than sacrifice, *and* to hearken than the fat of rams (1 Samuel 15:22, KJV)."

This journey hasn't been easy, but it's been worth it. God has taught me a lot; He has formed me into a beautiful butterfly. I went through a lot because of my choices. I caused myself pain because I would not humble myself. My test and trials were teaching me, so I can give wisdom to all women; young and old.

I must admit, my flesh was my downfall. I have fought the wrong fights and fought the wrong people. I am so glad I have matured to be great and let things of the past go. I am a **Survival Kit Woman**. I survived my journey.

6

ANSWERED THE CALL

I attended Apostle Futch's church in Glennville. He licensed me as an Evangelist on February 3, 2013. I was called to Pastor in March of 2013 and ordained in November of 2013. God did a quick work in me because he needed me. I answered the call and didn't care who thought I was not worthy of it.

This book is a part of my testimony, and there is more to come. I am a woman with many weaknesses who loves God. The devil wants my soul, my purpose, and he cares nothing about me, but God is my protection. We must humble ourselves, learn to listen, and take correction. Teenagers, honor your parents. Single moms who are reading this book, I made it with the help of the Lord. Don't give up on your dreams; change your life for your children. God pulled me through the roughest stages of my life. He was my husband, my protector, and my strength. I changed my life, and I see the fruits of my labor. All my children are called to ministry. I didn't know who I was raising until I gained a relationship with God.

Let Jesus be your personal savior, "If thou confess with thy mouth the Lord Jesus, and shalt believe in thine heart that God hath raised him from the dead, thou shalt be saved (Romans 10:9, KJV)." For all of you single, saved, and struggling women, I ask that you love God first. If you are struggling with flesh, God can and will deliver you. It took years for me to get there, but I'm there now. Hallelujah! It is not easy but through fasting and praying, it is possible.

My Next book: <u>The Dark Side in Ministry Being a Single, Beautiful, and Attractive Pastor.</u>

About the Author

Pastor Cynthia was born in Glennville, Georgia. Everything she learned came from the streets of Glennville, which taught her how to survive. Pastor Cynthia overcame many obstacles by listening and maturing in the areas where she was weak. Her darkest moments and the life she lived became her testimony! The enemy set many traps, but God spared her life because he had a purpose and a plan. The end.

www.ingramcontent.com/pod-product-compliance
Lightning Source LLC
LaVergne TN
LVHW011431080426
835512LV00005B/381